Here Beyond Small Wonders

poems by

Becky Boling

Finishing Line Press
Georgetown, Kentucky

Here Beyond Small Wonders

Copyright © 2025 by Becky Boling
ISBN 979-8-88838-933-1 First Edition
All rights reserved under International and Pan-American Copyright Conventions. No part of this book may be reproduced in any manner whatsoever without written permission from the publisher, except in the case of brief quotations embodied in critical articles and reviews.

Publisher: Leah Huete de Maines
Editor: Christen Kincaid
Cover Art: Becky Boling
Author Photo: Steve Maus
Cover Design: Elizabeth Maines McCleavy

Order online: www.finishinglinepress.com
also available on amazon.com

Author inquiries and mail orders:
Finishing Line Press
PO Box 1626
Georgetown, Kentucky 40324
USA

Poems

Tornado	1
Swept Away	2
Stag	4
Adirondack Chair in Snow	5
Rescued	6
Snow Pond	8
Resurrection of Green	10
Bruin in a Cold Stream	11
Small Wonders	12
Icebox	13
dead mouse	15
Musca Domestica: An Elegy	16
A Large Black Ant	17
Owls	18
Blue Jay	21
Melt	22
Inland Sea	23
Greenheads	25
Sunset on Lake Michigan	26
Clothesline	27
Horse Fly	28
The Mutiny of Walnuts	29
An End-of-Summer Gala	30
Persephone's Bouquet	31
Diminishment of Days	35
squatters	36
Hummingbird on the Hudson	38
Ash and Bone	39

Garden of Benign Neglect 40

A Garden Between Walls 41

With or Without Us 43

A Lake in a Forest 44

Drowned 46

Green Gifts 47

shores 48

blue 50

A Land Emergent 51

Acknowledgments 52

For Doug and Zach

Tornado

I live in tornado alley at the northern tip but was born in the southern grip
of the Ohio Valley, where heated river currents spawn torrential
funnels that churn fields, wood, concrete, and steel.

That was where I learned to ride the twister's tail—
those great serpentine winds—to let them blow
through me, to open like the windows
and doors of our house as the vigor
and drama sank through skin
and muscle, slid over bones
and blew away like demons
from a nightmare.

The twisting tail drilled roots in soil that it wasn't meant for
and in its cycling coils, it swept away both the dead
and the living, both loose particles of tilled soil not
yet planted, seeds not yet rooted, the dreams
of some and the lives, too, leaving no
promise that it would not
come again.

I learned to ride the green
sky and bear the nearness
of Armageddon like
those of us who
were born in
the serpent's
path.

Swept Away

That winter night, blue and frosty,
when I got into my rusty Dodge Dart
eager to spend the weekend with you,
I wasn't thinking of snow-iced roads
or blinding, glazed windowpanes
but warm laughter, hands reaching,
whispered moments on cotton pillowcases,
our complicit adolescent bodies
on the verge of adulthood—you
in your first real job, I still
in school—folding like mirror images,
one into another, the heart of sameness.

The single-lane highway threaded
west to the state line. I clutched
the wheel, fingers numb, checked
the temperature of the arctic gale
billowing from the heat vents.
Shivers along my back chipped
with an ice pick at my self-delusion.
The forced air was no warmer.

The second- or third-hand car my mother
had bought me when I turned eighteen
came without a manual, without frills,
familiar switches, levers, or dials.
Only later, when winter gave a dying roar,
would I learn how to turn on the heat.

On worn treads, I glided into the last town
my side of the border, not far from the city
where you had set up house.
I drove down a neighborhood street,
through an arboreal tunnel. Canopies
of bare branches arched and stretched
overhead, a thousand arms embraced,
despite the span of sidewalk and pavement.

Sifted snowflakes glimmered beneath
street lamps as they floated towards me,
before they could find rest on my windshield.
My headlights parted the wintery veil.
Powdery particles, far too light to resist
the gentle brush of wipers, fell
to either side of the road,
swept into the darkness.

That moment endures, a memory
that comes each winter when I drive in snow.
I watch, suspended, while snow winnows itself,
clears a path before me that still waits in patient
calm and splendor, knowing you are waiting, too.

A bower of white crystals falls, like a sacrament,
on the threshold of a life. I am already nostalgic
for what is passing, has passed, resigned
to the inevitable, but no longer able to feel the cold.

Stag

Eyes caught in headlight
on a tar-dark county road,
his breath smudges the night
with a moist white mist.

Clutching the steering wheel,
I watch the standing stag.
I am caught by the same awe,
he by the light, I by his grandeur.

He turns, majestic, bounds,
a blur of brown fur, far
from road to midnight field,
a contrail of dancing antlers.

Adirondack Chair in Snow

Outside my mother's apartment building,
the Adirondack chair wears a winter mantle,
its back, armrests, and seat piled with snow,
all four legs gone, as if amputated,
wedged deep into the snowbank.

A chair for lakefront cabins, for warm
days and nights, a chair immune to rain,
the Adirondack is outside its element.

What good's a chair
in so wintery a setting?
Manufactured by and for us,
it poses as a garden ornament,
a bucket for shovelfuls of snow.
We should be sitting there.
But the blizzard scurried us indoors—
the Adirondack chair buried
in frigid banks, forgotten.

This chair recalls laps
we once knew, strong arms
to buttress childish bodies,
a breast we nestled against.

Mother's moved on.
We sweep history
from her place,
ready it for another.

Snow-covered, the chair
shivers at her absence.

Rescued

Summers ago, I bought them—
two coleuses striated greens, purples, reds,
visitors to my garden,
a last cry of summer in August's heat.

I set them side by side
in the orange basin of an ancient
wheelbarrow that leaned
seductively against the walnut tree.

Cheap, the coleuses came late,
annuals meant to last a season.
I watched them in their setting.
Summer waned, they did not.
Their painted leaves brightened
even the walnut's shade.

As fall hovered and temps dipped,
the two plants, potted sentinels,
refused to surrender,
kept their post,
resplendent and thick leaved.

Tenacious, proud, and vain,
two coleuses, doomed to shrivel
and die with the season.

One crisp autumn morn,
spying them still vibrant
in their summer clothes,
I scooped them from their stations,
rushed them inside
to shelter from the cold,
convinced they would languish
and slip away quietly
from day to day.

Now in their second winter,
I water dark soil in tiny pots.
In awe, I witness
small leaves bud along their stems.
Lithe branches fork and stretch
against the windowpane,
remembering late summer's sun.

Snow Pond

The melted snow pond
in our backyard
froze again overnight.
White shock lines—
like starbursts—
fan out from trunks of captive trees.
The plastic green rim
of a capsized lawn chair
juts out of an ice-covered bog.

Staring through glass panes
from my warm dining room,
surrounded by walls, bookcases,
privileged plants in decorative pots,
table and chairs varnished smooth,
I am assailed by images that melt
on the tongue like last week's
snowflakes, struck by a landscape
put on pause by fickle temperatures
and unerring laws of science.

Poetry, like freezing temps,
seizes the moment, recasts
it—through the physics of sight,
memory, language—resurrects
it anew into patterns,
sound and light,
marks on a snowy page
that glisten and melt on tongue,
alight on the inner eye.

What I see, though I have seen
it in other guises time after time,
astounds me still with its alchemy,
the mutation of seeds that burst into flower,
pumpkins sprouting into carriages,
fat honey bees' impossible pirouettes,
reedy breath trembling into song.

I open myself to a pool of words,
as the slick immobility of ice
over the flooded yard
shimmers, melts, then crystallizes,
dappling the white sheet.

Resurrection of Green

And because snow
believes in spring
in resurrection of green
diminished domain of ice,
light's rebellious rays
return to melt winter's reign.

Bruin in a Cold Stream

Is it a boulder or a brown bear?
The spray from the stream
dapples my lenses with spots.
A stippled play of shadows
from the spindly trees
on the rocky overhang
etches lines, draws an ear,
carves the curve
of a bruin's humped back.
She has fallen asleep
as the cascade boils
and roils around her,
bisecting diaphanous waters
falling, frigid and frothy,
from White Mountain's
snowy peak, a melt-off
whose shivering fingers
comb the thick warm nap
of her winter coat.
Frothy white foam
shampoos her russet fur,
washes away burs, twigs,
the grit of hibernation.
I hear her sigh
over the rumble
of currents, envy
her calm stillness.
She knows the fish
will always come,
knows the sleep
she now gives into
is brief, the cold
nothing more
than a soothing respite
in spring's warm welcome.

Small Wonders

Here beyond small wonders,
a million insects argue and play.

Their yellow fire travels sky and time
against indifference, asking,
others so do say, to go a different way,
a final creation to prepare,
to set an early eve ablaze.

I, at sleep, swathed in midnight cloth
hear the world crowd in toward day.
Next to me, a shiny blue-winged victim
beats back the terrors of creation.

Icebox

In the backyard
under the only tree we had
where my mom and grandma parked their rusty cars
there was an old icebox, squat and fat,
open door hanging askew.

My grandma had it dropped there
to make room for the new Frigidaire.
A house of women
we didn't haul large appliances
to the dump.

We didn't own a truck.

I crept to the open maw of that old icebox
left to molder and rust under a tree.
I recalled warnings of children
trapped inside. They suffocated
playing hide and seek in the city garbage dump
unable to open the door,
unable to make themselves heard.

In the shade of our dwarfed sycamore,
the appliance became a portal to a dark region,
the kind that cobwebbed dreams.
I expected to hear the moans
of the dead, to smell the sulfur
of regret as I drew near, at least
the stale reek of old cheese
and soured milk.

I found instead a diaphanous shroud
woven of thin filaments
crisscrossing the dark
opening,
a web to ensnare
Orpheus
on his bootless return,
to punish

his lack of faith,
his impatient desire.

Before my fingers reached out
to touch the spidery veil,
the threads' vibrations
led me to the center.

There, patience itself,
the spider,
guard and keeper,
its delicate legs
strumming the strings,
enthralled me.

dead mouse

my dog still young knows the smell of carrion
he nuzzles his way through damp
leaves and woodchips
burrows into bushes that still sleep
storing sap for a spring too early to trust

when he backs out, I know with a sense
perhaps learned or just there all along—
instinct not unlike his, perhaps mirroring his own
with a call and response

I am sure that he has found it, the dead thing
that crawled into safety too late
who curled like a fetus or stretched on its side
and died alone in the muck

Musca Domestica: An Elegy

The sun irradiates the room,
heating the composite surface
of counters, desks, and shelves.

Blinds cut light into oblique
rays that strafe my desk,
emblazoning a thin veil of dust.

Wayward flies lost on currents
of human-scented air, slip past us
before doors snap shut,

spiral up stairwells, a quest
for food, air, egress. Doomed,
they haunt corridors, classrooms.

Careless crumbs plot a course.
On desperate wings, they ascend
higher into the maze until

they reach the farthest corner,
breach my open door, drum, bodies
heavy, on windows' slick glass.

Here stayed, they pine for open skies,
branching trees, and green fields
on the other side of a closed window.

They come to my office, expect
escape, but find only an illusion
beyond reach. They beat their wings,

hour after hour, sadden, then fall
to the windowsill to die
among those that came before.

A Large Black Ant

Today I took a shower with a large black ant.

I didn't know I had company until the end
when I grabbed my towel and glanced down
to see a blurry black curl opposite the drain.

Myopic, I thought it a clump of hair or a bit of fuzz
from the sweater I've been clinging to these days
for comfort against late spring coolness
as well as the tedium of isolation from the pandemic.

There, curled like a macaroni—
perhaps similar to the day
he came into this world—
the intrepid scout for his colony.
What watery message
might he have sent to the nest
before he died?

Did my soapy ablutions give him time
to warn his kin of the cataracts of doom
the slick cliffs rising vertical in all directions
the roaring whirlpool in the center of the world
that dragged everything down between the colossal
columns of the evil giant who lives here?

Owls

I

The owls were out
in the tree yesterday.
People milled around,
tugged on recalcitrant dogs,
herded flocks of children.

Heads turned at uncomfortable
angles, knees and feet
wobbled for purchase.
We stared through leaves,
infused life into crisscrossed
limbs and gnarled wood
until at last we honed in
on the objects of our gaze.

Above us,
wings flexed,
heads swiveled,
cautious inhuman eyes
stared down at us.

        Predators, aren't we all?

Why do we stand, transfixed?
Risk vertigo? Swaying
branches rock us on our heels.
To catch a glimpse
of a raptor and its young?

What drama is this that does
not so much unfold as stop
time in freeze frames,
leaving us to spin on our axis—
vibrations on a taut wire?

We long to transgress
the urban landscape,
escape the squared
corners of our edifices,
the flat pavement of our roads.

II

On greened branches
downy-backed owlets
test claws, practice
silence and stealth
in plain view.

The show begins,
audience rapt, necks craned.

From their wooden hollow,
peer fuzzy-winged raptors.
We hold our breath.
I-phones digitalize,
post and share,
frame by frame,
their frozen stare.

Flotsam caught in the eddy
of a stream, couples, families,
lone walkers, eyes tangled
in the canopy, anticipate the scene.
Some drift off, others arrive,
search for the best angle.
Clustered beneath the boughs,
we whisper, testify, conjecture,
bit players awaiting our cue.

An adult owl hovers
several trees distant,
emits a deep throaty call
a febrile, high double-time note,

an invisible tether flung
over our pivoting heads
to the nest above.

III

Where?
Fingers point.
Eyes strain.
Each visit requires
a new orientation.

We share the role of guide,
inheriting knowledge,
passing it on.

There. Alone the owlets,
less fuzz, more wing,
move about in patterns
up, down, across.
No one stands guard,
except those of us
who come each day,
to mark their change.

Soon, we say, we'll come
to find them gone.

Blue Jay

A slice of sky, he
lights on my porch.

Between blue spandrels
and carved peach spindles
framed. A royal profile
from sweeping blue crest
to sleek black beak
he poses, all stillness.

There he perches
as if the trim on my porch
were a tree limb, birch or oak.

Sable stripes on a blue canvas
about the eye, on wing,
distinguish him from sky.

His mate flits by, too quick
for sight, except as shadow
across porch then skyward
beyond my window frame.

Blue jay rests blue on blue
a moment more, then off—
blue into blue.

Melt

Summer bears down on the city like granny's old quilt.
On elbows and forearms, I hang over the balcony.
My potted ferns swoon in the corner, out of breath.
Eyes closed, attuned to a second skin of sweat,
I stretch neck and torso, searching for a cool
note rising from the street below.
My rainbow sherbet melts cold comfort,
drips onto my pup's hot tongue.

Inland Sea

They built a wooden staircase
to protect the sand and grass
against our transgressions

I walk out of the forest
to descend to foaming lake water
story by story, step by step

right angle wooden slats
bow, groan, and crack
splinters wait for careless hands

I count step after step
in each set of stairs
eleven here, thirty there

each summer I lose track
passing seventy, eighty,
ninety steps and more

flight after flight
pulled toward the sea-blue
expanse of water below

buffeted by wind
blasted by sun
I pause midway

down the final staircase
I catch my breath
and forget to count

before my heavy tread
reaches the searing sand
that burns the bottoms of my soles

before the sharp edges
of beach grass prick
and gouge my instep

before my toes clutch
the polished stones
of Michigan's inland sea

Greenheads

When the wind dies
and the sun fires
the beach without pity,
horse flies, green heads
glistening in the sun,
rise from whispering
reeds of bladed dune grass
to strafe in midday heat
Michigan's sandy shore.

Sunset on Lake Michigan

Cobalt blue water churns
and shivers in autumn cold.

There have been shipwrecks
on this inland sea. And yet

sunsets fire the sky and airy
currents rise wet, spreading

thick a pomegranate red
capped by smoky purple clouds.

Summer bathers are gone, releasing
the lake to its own rhythmic course.

Light splinters its spectrum
into waves that break—
blue, yellow, red—and crash against

a vacant shore. Shards of color
dissolve and saturate air, water, sand.

The breadth of drenched beach
shimmers florescent under slants
of gradient light. Sand turns

to glass, refracting the blinding gold
of our somnolent star as it drifts
from sky, lake, and horizon.

Beauty too vast
for the eye to grasp. No
wonder sunsets slip so quickly away.

No wonder I return, like those waves,
to stare out at the world's end in wonder.

Clothesline

I

Splayed and clipped to a languid line,
beach towels dance the seven veils,
stripes undulating, colors streaming

buffeted by summertime breezes,
buoyed on watery ebb-and-flow dreams.

Sand dries and scatters, pitched like seeds
into the wind while cool damp undersides
and hot dry swaths of cloth skim sunlight,

snap and flick out the impress of body weight,
aerating the yard with suntan emollients,

lotion's chemical perfume, sweat,
and the fishy tang of the inland sea.

II

When wind dies like the sun that slips
beneath the bowed horizon, so, too,

the waft and pitch of each long lumbering
length of cloth abates. Clip after clip, I collect

fields of colors—tangerine, cloud, sun, sky,
and ruby. Limp and heavy, the towels tumble

like weary babes into my open arms
to be folded and tucked in for the night.

Horse Fly

The horse fly, the biting kind,
chose to dine on me that July
on the Michigan lakefront beach.

I was the morsel on a sandy plate
of charcuterie, a sunbaked savory
sweat-seasoned in the mid-summer heat.

From the dune grass, she came,
green head, razor mouth, to eat
or die, ravenous for her blood feast.

Midday sacrifice, driven mad
by a dauntless pursuer, I dove
bleeding into cold lake water.

Somewhere, in the tall grass
or heavy on the windless air,
she waits for dessert.

The Mutiny of Walnuts

The first to go are the walnuts.
They send out gold parchment leaves,
missives of premature warning.
Under their branches, they weave of the lawn
a patchwork of yellow and green.
This mutiny is too early. Swiveling
my porch chair to face away from them,
I reject this ambivalent Minnesota August,
one foot in summer, the other in autumn.

When I was a child deep in the Ohio valley,
in the southern dripping toe of Indiana,
August was the month of sweltering heat,
river-heavy air, and drowsy fat flies.

Shame on you, Walnuts, for your haste.
You are too easily swayed by a cooling breeze.

August nights are not so cold, the days
stretch far into the evening hours.
We buy sweet corn and watermelons
from the back of a farmer's truck.
No call for jack-o-lanterns or caramel apples.
The luminous spark of fireflies still dots the night.
Summer may yet gild the fields and feed the songbird.
O, Walnuts! Keep your leaves a while longer.

An End-of-Summer Gala

It rained, then stopped, as if it knew
we would like to sit out on the porch.
A late August wind banks the sun's fire
sifted and cooled through streaks of cloud,
dappled and splayed through green canopies.

We venture out and watch the dusky play
of slanting light beneath darkling trees,
listen to the first strains of orchestral hymns
stirred by the grace of supple limbs—
swaying like a conductor's baton—
streaming a woody score through reedy leaves.

From the shaded undergrowth
bursts a diurnal chorus of stridulating cicadas
droning their shrill relentless note,
like a dying operatic diva
who refuses to leave the stage,
a fitting aria for summer's last gala.

Persephone's Bouquet

I

Colors—
veins, dark green
lines of forests
etched,
the maple's cellular
destiny.
Water-colored
canvases
wind-blown
scarlet, earth,
on the lawns
still green
late to autumn's
feast of famine.
Singed tips
fold like newborn
fingers
grasping
for life
crumpling
in upon leaf's palm.

II

I'm a kid
despite three decades
short of a century.
On my walk
in oblique sunshine,
I can't decide—
look up or down,
surrounded, as
I am, by arboreal
love letters pinned
to tree limbs,
others loose
and scattered

on a yet green
canvas—
hot-pepper reds
creamy yellows
summer's cool
sap seeping away
to the edges,
rousted by dawn's
orange brightness,
others a brazen scarlet
rare purples. And
one midnight leaf,
whose darkness
mystifies.
Has it absorbed
the sun's palette,
famished
for light?

III

Orange—
too simple a word,
a compromise
between red and yellow,
or a ghostly brown
in darkening veins,
an orange
true flame's
flicking whips
of light and heat.
Tangerine and citrus
too bright, orange,
too plain,
like a child's
box of crayons.

IV

I pluck the fallen
from sidewalks,
lawns, press
crescent stems
between thumb
and forefinger,
like a matron
of honor
under autumn's
cathedral dome
as Persephone
descends,
silent footfalls
on crushed
leaves.
I choose
my bouquet,
scalloped
or serrated
margins,
one for desire,
its fiery embers
yet burning;
ginger-orange
to spice the air
for cinnamon
pleasures
of shared bounty;
the spray of cut citrus
like laughter, for my loves'
joy infusing
all my days and nights,
the memory of cool
pulp at the bottom
of the cup
for gratitude;
a last one

for forgiveness
whose yellow rays
of sun sweep
the dark ashes
from my doorway.

Diminishment of Days

I wear the diminishment of days
with varying degrees of grace.
Some days, I choose a hairshirt
to scratch away the scales.
Sometimes, a summer
shift lies on me
silken, like
endless
days.

squatters

squatters we lease our land from rabbits
we peer from makeshift homes
patched and painted
tricolored façades
Victorian farm houses
built circa 1890
the last nail struck
before the turn of a foregone century
before great-great grandma's first child
on land that hemmed the valley
distant from town halls
general stores
and grain elevators
above the floodplain
of an oblivious river

we leave baby carrots
on back porch steps
peeled and whittled
to pinky proportions
packaged and trucked
cold to the touch
meant for dips and snacks
they shrivel and rot
while rabbits forage
among weedy plots
through spiky shoots of grass
gnawing at roots and stalks

this side of gray metallic screens
on a thrice-built back porch
we watch mottled short-eared hares
nibble at untended gardens
feast among peonies
creeping charlie
gnarled lilacs and bottlebrush sedge
that came with a thirty-year mortgage
like arthritic floorboards
and asthmatic pipes

the legacy of other occupants
who lie in stone gardens under
mounds of earth

former tenants
with greener thumbs
who passed this way
dropping seeds
burying bulbs
over long-forgotten beds
of bitter rhubarb
fields of spuds
and sweeps of
wild onion
wherein rabbits gorge

Hummingbirds on the Hudson

In 1851, Putnam published *Rural Hours* by a Lady
and the Hudson River Railroad pulled ninety tons
of iron and steam from New York City to Poughkeepsie.

Winged, needle-beaked, the hummingbird fades
in water color stains, reds turned rusty, greens dull.

It flutters on the wafting floral bouquet,
a fragrant seduction of blooms in a garden.

The tiny flyer sucks on honey-suckle goblets
overflowing with the wine of summer nectar.

Light as light itself, heart tripping in fairy tap time
a lady's thoughts hummingbird their way over an emerald
meadow or slip inside a secret garden

beneath a cottage's watchful eye, skim along an abandoned plot
dotted with wild abandon by thistles, scrub grass,
a thousand shades of salvia and vagrant bee balm.

The smallest of birds whisks silken on whispered
sighs, ferried by a lover's breath, a lady's smile.

Red-throated, it hovers, fragile, the hummingbird
in the path of a rumbling iron beast
belching flames and smoke. Metal tracks shriek and spark
igniting the sky, burning its gossamer wings.

In long flowing letters, a lady flits among words,
captures the delicate aerobatics of iridescent wings
in rhyme and story, a tale of airy flights embossed
on folded, stitched sheets, a lady lost in honeysuckle.

In the distance, the rumble, hiss, and screech of metal
and the acrid smell of steam.

Ash and Bone

a core irony of Earth
we're too willful to learn:
we sign the deed, wave the mortgage
pierce the soil with steel and concrete roots
carve a name in deep furrows beneath our yoke
we shingle the landscape in dead trees
excavate, extract, and bull-doze
our way, like infection
in a wound that festers
spreading and burrowing
running from sunrise, rushing
to sunset, we drive stakes
draw borders and etch our initials
parceling longitude and latitude
we scowl at mountain ranges
and christen totemic towers
that rise like stalagmites
to butcher the blue of the sky
we speak of legacy
and the land we own
we who end
as so much ash
and bone

After "Hamatreya" by Ralph Waldo Emerson

Garden of Benign Neglect

We bought a garden
that came with a house.
We bought it in summer
when rose bushes bloomed.

Robins and sparrows gathered
at feeders, waded through
rainbow pools in terra cotta basins.

The elm hovered above house and yard,
gathered us like errant chicks under its bower,
ferried squirrels from canopy to canopy,
sifted sunshine and raindrops over us all.

But we had no talent at green things,
no patience with suet and sunflower seeds.

We pulled out sprouting clumps of green
assuming they were weeds.
We showered our yard
with haphazard love and awkward attention.

Like unreliable parents,
we gave too little too late.

We still have the house,
but the garden has retreated,
giving way to the hardier,
more common, grass-like growths.

Birds fly by on their way
to more hospitable dwellings.
Our diseased elm was euthanized,
its remains long ago carted off.

We don't know the names of what's left.
They come and go as they please.
Fortunate, they have no need of us.

A Garden Between Walls

Soil ignores the blue painted wall
with its graffiti of tropical greens
and sunburnt salamanders, a postcard
nostalgia for distant rain forests.

A neighborhood garden grows
between buildings whose foundations
dig down as deep as the fibrous
roots of a century old oak.

Like sugar or salt, granulated
earth, raked and hoed for planting
in the neighborhood garden,
crumbles and flows,
filling the void,
a black river of detritus
processed from any and all
glorious organic matter,
rotting and seething,
redolent in nutrients
stewed and seeping
from kitchen garbage:
tossed rinds, coffee grounds,
egg shells, the scum
from unwashed plates.

This cyclical composted waste
ferments to feed life
from a thousand comestible deaths.

Two-, four- and six-legged creatures
run, scramble, burrow along pathways
in terrestrial cities within cities
stealing from steel and concrete
a cultivated natural ecosystem
open to rain and sunlight
under the care of community—

a few hours a day to grow a radish
to nourish tomatoes and eggplant
to weed carrots, cucumber
and vining beans—

a stolen, rescued Eden
framed between brick
asphalt and cement,
rising from the loamy cracks
of a city landscape.

With or Without Us

We are not necessary to the maple
nor to the forsythia that blooms.

White crocuses and blue squill burst
through to a warming world alit with sun.

Whether we languish or thrive,
the cardinal mocks us with bright color.

Around us birdsong drowns our woe
but does not sing of our plight.

Wind still sweeps fields and forests
though all but a few planes sit grounded.

Sun warms or slips behind rain clouds
as the battery in my watch slowly drains.

Rivers swell rushing to the sea
harboring and nourishing life along their way.

Summer will come, fall with follow
winter will whisper the world to sleep.

And with or without us spring will come again.

A Lake in a Forest

What is it about a lake in a forest
that despite gritty banks,
mosquitoes, chilled breezes
draws us to breathe soggy air
and wood smoke?

We settle into a rustic cabin
on a lakeshore nestled
within the arms of a forest,
disregard grimy floor boards,
the stew of cedar, citronella,
and damp sofa cushions.

Descending the mossy ladder,
we propel ourselves into water,
stare down a dark well
to a bottomless basin.

The sun courses overhead,
dips behind the woods,
leaving us in secondhand
light, borrowed shade.

Far from dock and shore, we tread,
bob like lost corks on the surface.

A needle-bodied dragonfly
helicopters above us,
lands on the island of our bare
heads, mistaking us for storm debris,
an airstrip for a brief layover
as it hunts lesser flying insects.

Water envelops us,
as we float, gives way
to our strokes like turned soil
to a sharp blade.

In a forest, air is more like air.

We hike through fields of trees
on dirt paths woven with nettles,
over gnarled roots, across
outcroppings of naked boulders
whose rounded shoulders
make us dream of sleeping giants.

Like dirty clothes, we cast aside
our city roles, play at adventure,
pretend to be experts with paddles
and canoes and sometimes
we make it to the island out there, sit
shivering on its pebbled beach, eat
packed sandwiches and drink
clean water we ferried from kitchen
faucets or 7 Elevens.

We ogle, in awe, at caravans
of ducklings and mother that sail
under the pier, the reed-legged heron
searching for toads amid lily pads and reeds,
the spider's air sack as the creature water-skis
over ripples; we sway to the whir
of cicadas, the woodwind song
of the loon, the crackle of the forest floor.

What is it about a lake in a forest
that takes the city out of the woman,
the woman out of the girl,
webs fingers and toes and makes
her walk barefoot over pebbles and needles?

What sylvan magic roots inside our souls,
soaks through our skin and eddies in our pores,
makes bearable our exile
amid pavement and gearshifts,
changes time, bends light,
and smooths the wrinkles of life?

Green Gifts

When the ice recedes
and earth groans under new wounds,
when forests go quiet
because monsters
encased in metal
excavate roots and saw
through living tissue,
when even the chemistry
of oceans, winds, soil
turns against seedlings
embryos, green shoots,
to redefine life itself,
we may wonder
why we craned necks
to stare at skyscrapers,
shielding eyes
from an angry sun
and why asphalt,
concrete, steel, and brick
were chosen to carpet
the landscape instead of cool, dry needles,
damp soil, clover, prairie grasses,
and warm beach sand.
Then, we may wish
we had blended in with the breathing world,
stretching limbs toward sky
to mimic the work of oak, birch, white pine
or closed each other in warm embrace
like those flowers whose blooms
fold for the night and wait for day.
When the world is past
caring for us, we might
wish we had cared more for green gifts
and the beating heart of companion souls.

Drowned
    For Marie

The drowned belong to the lake where they died.
They slumber weightless on a bed of silt.
Fanned by ferns, kissed by shoals of limpid fish,
they need no words nor breath yet sometimes sigh.

They hear children splash in the shallows,
the whir of hungry dragonflies in flight,
frogs on lily pads croaking for lost loves.

When dappled ripples reflect the moon's crest,
they hear a lone loon's tremolo far away,
the cry of an owl's prey from the forest.

The drowned belong to the lake where they died,
forget that once they were fished from the deep,
bewitched by the lake's liquid lullaby,
rocked in cool soothing arms that promised sleep.

shores

emergent crust, jutting rock
chunk of sub-continental land
isle, islet, skerry, or cay

how large the mass, how great
the width or coastline shore

oasis in sea-salt waters
or wrinkle that splits a river
or crowns a lake's complacence

island bejeweled by pastel coral
reefs feasted upon by anime fish
washed in Warhol pigments

island chains like paving stones
tip-toe over briny seas
glisten on slick covers
of travel brochures

otherworldly, dreamscapes
for city-locked tourists avid
for pineapples, tropical limes
crab succulent over smoking pits

island of imagination, lands
of wet, shifting borders

island, bite-sized continent
land contiguous with sea floor
coast, beach, mountain, plain

no one, Donne tells us, is an island
each of us born of blood, flesh
rent from our mother's womb
we land, wet, writhing

on the shore, this rock
or that sandy holm
on the soft belly of our world

into those hands that fold
us to earth's bounty

no one is
but becomes
no one is
but comes to this island—
this blue gem—in a dark universe

we shipwrecked islanders
washed up on this shore

blue

between wing
rain
and drunk winter

we think time slow
as eye drinks
smooth blue depths

between wing
rain
and drunk winter

A Land Emergent

Dolphins caress my inner thighs
with velvet-slick skin while sea otters
and seals slide in riots down my shins
to dive blind into lilac-scented water.

Schools of shy fish idle in the concave
depths of my armpits while eels spiral
my wrists in silver bands of light.

Faint with steam and weightless in the tub,
I slide my foot along the smooth enamel basin.
My leg bends and emerges into the cool air.
A boney island redoubt, my knee juts
above the surface, waves breaking all around me.

I gather the world, flesh bounded by water and air—
an archipelago risen
from the depths
a clustering of protuberances
in an aquatic sphere.

Upon the promontory of my thigh
a sister mermaid reclines,
tail fin stirring the bluish, soapy bath.
A song slips wet from her lips to coil
damp and heavy along my limbs.

I am a land submerged, alive
with kinetic power, mother
of cataclysmic births and rebirths
maker of shores, cliffs, and entire continents
teased by the fluttering undercurrents
of whale songs and coral dreams.

Acknowledgments

I wish to acknowledge and express my gratitude to the following publishers of my poems.

Willows Wept Review: "Tornado," "Swept Away," "Adirondack Chair in Snow," "Snow Pond," "dead mouse," "Owls," "Clothesline," "squatters," "Garden of Benign Neglect," "A Lake in a Forest," and "Drowned"

Martin Lake Journal: "Stag"

Red Wing Arts' Poet-Artist Collaboration: "shores"

Visual Verse: Anthology of Art and Words: "Tornado," "A Garden Between Walls," "Hummingbird on the Hudson," "A Land Emergent"

We Look West Poets of the Northfield Public Library: "Swept Away" "Icebox"

Little by Little, the Bird Builds Its Nest. Paris Morning Publications: (2024) "Blue Jay" and "Owls"

Born in Evansville on the banks of the Ohio in Southern Indiana, **Becky Boling** earned a B.A. from the University of Southern Indiana, an M.A. from ISU in Terre Haute, and then moved to Chicago to complete her Ph.D. at Northwestern University. For thirty-six years at Carleton College in Northfield, Minnesota, she taught Spanish language and Latin American literature and led several student programs to Morelia, Mexico. She married, raised a family with her poet husband, D. E. Green, and has written short stories, novels, creative nonfiction, dramatic monologues, and poetry. The Stephen R. Lewis, Jr. Professor of Spanish and the Liberal Arts, Emerita, Boling has published in *Lost Lake Folk Opera, Willows Wept Review, Persimmon Tree, 3rdWednesday Magazine, Misfit, The Ekphrastic Review, Moss Puppy, Visual Verse: Anthology of Art and Words, Gleam: Journal of the Cadralor* and *Agates.* Her poems have been recognized as part of the Northfield Sidewalk Poetry project and Red Wing Arts' Poet-Artist Collaboration (2020, 2022). Twice she has been nominated for a Pushcart Prize. MPR's *Pandemic Poetry* has featured her poems, and her work appears in Ramsey County Library's *This Was 2020: Minnesotans Write About Pandemics and Social Justice in a Historic Year, We Look West* (Shipwreckt Books), *Bridge and Division* (Northfield Public Library), and *Little by Little, the Bird Builds Its Nest* (Paris Morning Press). *Here Beyond Small Wonders* is her first published book of poetry.

www.ingramcontent.com/pod-product-compliance
Lightning Source LLC
Chambersburg PA
CBHW030059170426
43197CB00010B/1591